# Contents

Words printed in the text in bold, **like this**, are explained in the Glossary.

The giant panda is one of the best-known animals in the world. Its appealing shape and black-and-white markings make it instantly recognizable, even though most people have never seen one. Unfortunately, pandas are also very rare and could soon die out. There are only about a thousand pandas in the world today. Scientists, governments and charities around the world are working hard to save them from **extinction**.

## Is it a bear?

The giant panda is a **mammal**, but for a long time scientists have disagreed about exactly which mammal family it belongs to. It looks like a bear, but it is mainly a plant-eater, while other bears are hunters.

The giant panda is related to the red or lesser panda, which looks like a raccoon, so some experts used to put the panda in the raccoon family.

The panda also shares some features with cats. For example, it has slit-shaped **pupils** in its eyes, and pads on its paws. The Chinese name for the panda, *Daxiongmao*, means 'large bear-cat'. Its scientific name is *Ailuropoda melanoleuca*, which is Latin for 'black and white cat-foot'. However, after recent tests on panda **DNA**, most scientists agree that pandas belong in the bear family or in a separate but closely related group.

*A female giant panda sitting in her mountain forest home in China, clutching a bamboo stem.*

## The other panda

The red panda or lesser panda (also known by its Latin name *Ailurus fulgens*) is related to the giant panda, but looks very different. It is much smaller – a giant panda can weigh up to 150 kilograms, but a red panda weighs only around 5 kilograms. The red panda has a long body like a raccoon, and reddish-brown fur. Like giant pandas, red pandas live in mountain forests in China and eat bamboo. They too are an endangered species.

A red panda, a much smaller relative of the giant panda.

## Discovering the panda

Pandas live in remote mountain forests in China. People there have known about giant pandas for thousands of years. In ancient China, panda fur was highly valued for keeping warm. A panda skull has even been found in the grave of an empress who was buried in the second century BC.

Even so, the outside world did not become familiar with pandas until the late 19th century. In 1869, a French **missionary** named Père Armand David saw a giant panda skin while visiting the house of a friend in the **Sichuan** region of China. On later visits, Père David managed to capture several pandas, and sent their skins and skeletons back to Europe to be studied. In the 20th century, people started to bring live pandas out of China to keep in zoos around the world.

In the 1970s and 80s, it became widely known that pandas were becoming endangered, and they became more and more popular. People flocked to zoos to see panda cubs born in **captivity**, and the panda became the symbol of the wildlife charity Worldwide Fund for Nature, or **WWF**.

# Where giant pandas live

The giant panda's natural home, or **habitat**, is high up in the mountains of central China, between 1000 metres and 4000 metres above sea level. Here, the slopes are covered with **conifer** trees and forests of bamboo, the panda's favourite food. The temperature is low and the weather can be misty, rainy or snowy. Pandas like damp surroundings, and usually live near mountain streams, springs or lakes.

Giant pandas like to live alone, except when they are **mating**, or when a mother is raising her cubs. Each panda has its own area, or **territory**, where it feeds and sleeps. The steep, rocky, densely forested hillsides allow pandas to hide away and keep to themselves.

However, over time, some of the forests have been cut down, and the land has been turned into farms or towns. This has forced pandas to move into remaining areas of forest, giving them less and less space to live in.

▲ *At some times of year, the mountains where pandas live can be cold and snowy. This panda is looking for food in deep snow.*

The following labels appear on the maps:

0 — 1000 kilometres

N

Panda distribution in 1800

Panda distribution today

RUSSIA

MONGOLIA

CHINA

INDIA

SOUTH CHINA SEA

CHINA

Beijing

Zhengzhou

Xi'an

SICHUAN PROVINCE

Chengdu

SOUTH CHINA SEA

*These maps show where pandas used to live 200 years ago and where they live now.*

# Changing conditions

Today wild pandas only live within a 13,000 square-kilometre area of forest covering six **isolated** mountain ranges in central China. In the past, their home **range** used to be much bigger. They may have lived across all of southeastern China, and possibly also in neighbouring countries such as Myanmar (Burma) and Vietnam. It is thought that their range may have shrunk partly because pandas like cool **climates**, and the climate of China may have once been cooler than it is now. As it warmed up, pandas were able to live only in higher mountain regions.

# Separate groups

As well as shrinking, the panda's natural habitat has been broken up into more than 30 separate areas of mountain forest. Low-lying areas and farms lie in between, splitting the wild panda population up into small groups. Known as **habitat fragmentation**, this makes it harder for pandas to move around to find food or meet a mate from another area.

# Giant panda populations

It is very hard to tell exactly how many giant pandas live in the wild. They are so rare and **solitary**, and live in such wild terrain, that it is difficult for scientists to find them and count them. One thing is for certain, though – there are not many pandas left.

These scientists are tracking a giant panda from footprints left in the snow.

In the mid-1980s, scientists held a panda **census**, which aimed to count how many pandas there were as accurately as possible. They calculated that there were about a thousand pandas living in the wild. Since that time, the panda's **habitat** has shrunk even more. But a new panda census, held in the years 2000–02, suggests that the panda population has not changed much in the last 20 years. There are probably still around a thousand giant pandas living in China's forests.

Besides those pandas that still live in the wild, there are also about 140 pandas that live in **captivity**, in **reserves** and research stations in China and in zoos around the world.

## Breeding problems

One of the problems facing pandas is that they **breed** very slowly. Even in perfect conditions, with plenty of space and a good choice of males to breed with, a female panda will usually only raise one cub at a time, and might only bring up two or three cubs in her lifetime. This means it takes a long time for pandas to build up their numbers.

With **habitat fragmentation**, it becomes even harder to breed. Animals need to move around and find **mates** from other areas. If animals mate with members of their own family, their offspring are more likely to have diseases and die young, because of the way **genes** – the instructions stored inside **cells** – are passed on. Animals are healthier if they have a mixture of different genes from different communities. Some **isolated** panda populations are made up of as few as 20 individuals, making it hard for each panda to find a suitable mate.

Pandas also seem to be very reluctant to breed in captivity. Although scientists and zoos try hard to breed more pandas as fast as they can, the world's tiny panda population is at a standstill. Unless we can find ways to help pandas to breed enough to increase their numbers again, they will continue to be at serious risk of dying out.

▶

*A mother giant panda at the Wolong Reserve, China, with her young cub. This cub, a male, is just three weeks old.*

## Six million to one

To get a sense of how few pandas there are in the world, think of it this way: there are a thousand giant pandas and more than 6 billion (6 thousand million) human beings in the world. This means that for every 6 million people on Earth, there is just one giant panda.

## Traditional tales

An old Chinese folktale gives an explanation for how the panda got its patterns. According to this legend, pandas used to be completely white. A young girl made friends with the pandas and saved a panda cub from being attacked by a leopard. In doing so she was fatally wounded, and the pandas went to her funeral. Weeping, they put their paws over their eyes and hugged themselves, leaving black marks on their fur which they have worn to this day.

Although related to bears, the giant panda looks unlike any other animal. Its body is specially **adapted** to its high mountain home, and over time it has developed many unique features.

Mountain weather can be cold and wet. Pandas have adapted to these conditions. While a panda may look soft and cuddly, the outer layer of its fur is very thick and coarse. This fur is covered in an oily, greasy substance produced by its skin. The oil keeps the fur waterproof, which is very important in such a wet **climate**. Underneath this is a layer of shorter, fluffier fur that traps air next to the panda's skin, helping it to keep warm.

Animals and people lose heat from the parts of their bodies that are in contact with the air. A panda's round, bulky body shape helps keep it warm. Compared to its size, very little of the panda's body is in contact with the air, so its body heat does not escape easily.

- Body length 1.5–1.8 m
- Height at shoulder 60–80 cm
- Adult males usually weigh 85–125kg though they can be more
- Adult females weigh 70–100kg

large head

slit-shaped pupils

sensitive nose and ears

strong teeth for chewing bamboo

black-and-white markings

plump, rounded body

thick, oily outer layer of fur

extra thumb designed for gripping bamboo

paws with pads on them

short tail

*In this picture you can see many of the giant panda's special body features.*

## In the dark

Pandas are crepuscular, which means they are most active at dawn and dusk. Sometimes they also have nocturnal, or night-time, feeding sessions. Although pandas do not have very good eyesight, their slit-shaped **pupils** can shrink or expand. This way they can let in more light at night, and less during the day. At night, pandas often use their excellent sense of smell to find food. They can also smell when another panda is nearby. Pandas have excellent hearing too, which helps them detect danger and other pandas.

## Panda patterns

Pandas are famous for their black-and-white markings. Although they have few natural enemies, experts think these patterns could have developed to give the panda **camouflage** in its rocky mountain home. The large black shapes help to break up the panda's outline, making it hard to see when it is sitting still against a background of rocks and trees. The black-and-white disguise would have been even more effective in the past, when the panda's **habitat** was colder and more snowy than it is today.

A giant panda feeding on bamboo. People can't help but find the large black eye markings appealing.

## Panda eyes

The large spot markings around its eyes help give the panda its attractive appearance, adding to its huge popularity. Humans find large eyes very appealing, as they remind us of young babies. However, pandas are not as cute as they seem. As many scientists have discovered, although pandas are not fierce, they have sharp claws and can bite very hard if they feel they are in danger.

# Food and feeding

The most important food for giant pandas is bamboo. Pandas do sometimes eat other foods, including flowers, berries, small animals such as mice and pikas (furry mountain **mammals** related to rabbits) and sometimes even fish. However, bamboo normally makes up at least 95 per cent of a wild panda's diet.

## Large lunch

Bamboo is a tall, thick, tough grass. Because most of a bamboo plant is made up of **fibre**, it contains very little useful **nutrition**. This means that pandas have to eat a huge amount of it to be healthy.

Pandas eat most parts of the bamboo plant, including the stalks, leaves and young shoots. In a typical day, a panda usually eats between 12 and 15 kilograms of bamboo. Some pandas have been known to eat up to 20 kilograms of bamboo in a day. That's at least ten times as much food as a person eats in a day, even though pandas and humans are similar in size. There are many different **species** of bamboo and pandas will eat several different types, but they prefer arrow bamboo and umbrella bamboo.

## When bamboo flowers

Unfortunately, the panda's favourite food plant, bamboo, has an unusual life cycle. Each bamboo plant spends most of its life growing only grassy leaves and stalks. Then, finally, it produces flowers, and later seeds, before dying. After a while, some of the seeds grow into new bamboo plants and the cycle begins again.

*A five-month-old panda cub chews some bamboo and plays in the snow after a fresh snowfall.*

Most types of bamboo live for between twelve and 20 years before flowering and dying, and some have a life cycle of over 50 years. But whenever they do finally flower and die, all the bamboo plants of the same species flower and die together. This means that a huge area of bamboo – which might be the main source of food for a whole population of pandas – can disappear all at once.

Hua mei, a panda at San Diego Zoo, California, USA, enjoys a special cake, made for her out of ice, bamboo and carrots, to celebrate her second birthday. Keepers give pandas ice to eat to help them keep cool.

## Feeding time at the zoo

Pandas living in **captivity** don't eat as much bamboo as in the wild, because it would be very hard for zookeepers to find all the bamboo they would need. Instead, captive pandas are fed on a mixture of other foods, such as rice, carrots, apples and honey, or on a special bread made of ground bamboo, rice and corn. The panda food also has **vitamins** added to make sure the pandas stay healthy.

## Designed for a bamboo diet

Pandas are perfectly **adapted** for eating bamboo. Their front paws have a unique 'extra thumb', which allows them to grasp a stalk of bamboo firmly. The thumb, called the radial sesamoid, is not a true thumb. It is a part of a panda's wristbone that has developed into an extra **digit**. Pandas usually eat sitting up, holding bamboo stalks in their front paws.

Because bamboo is so tough, pandas also have very big molars, or back teeth – five times the size of a human's molars – for grinding up bamboo stalks. Their jaw muscles also have to be very strong to crush the bamboo.

The panda's oesophagus (the tube that carries food to the stomach) has an extra-tough lining which may protect it from bamboo splinters. The panda's stomach also contains extra-strong muscles for mashing and **digesting** the bamboo.

# Giant pandas at home

Like many wild animals, pandas are **territorial**. This means that each giant panda has its own living space, or territory, which it patrols and guards from other pandas. Having a territory allows each panda to live by itself and find enough food in its own area.

A typical panda territory covers an area of around 3.5–6.5 square kilometres. Pandas mark their territories to show whom the area belongs to. They scratch and chew tree trunks, strip off pieces of bark, and rake the ground with their claws, so other pandas know whose territory it is.

## Smelly messages

Even more importantly, pandas mark their territories with smells. They use urine, droppings, and also a unique smelly substance which they make in a special **gland** beneath their tails. By rubbing their rumps on rocks and trees, and using their tails as a brush, they leave this smelly substance all around their territory. Experts think that pandas have such a good sense of smell that they can recognize each other by their scent.

Pandas spend a lot of time alone, but they do mingle to some extent, especially males. Male pandas have overlapping **ranges** which they do not defend, so they often wander into the ranges of other pandas. They may spend quite a lot of time in the home ranges of female pandas. Female pandas, on the other hand, do not like to mix with other females. Pandas call to each other using a bleating, yelping noise that some people say sounds like the cry of a human child.

*A resting panda uses her extra 'thumb' to hold on to a branch above her head.*

A young panda resting on the top of a tree stump at the Wolong Panda Research Centre in China.

## A place to rest

Apart from their territories, pandas do not have an actual home, such as a cave or burrow, except for females when giving birth. Instead, each panda spends its time wandering around its territory looking for food, and stopping to eat here and there. Although they can feed at any time of the day or night, pandas often do most of their feeding at dusk, dawn or night-time, and sleep for the main part of the day.

When a panda feels tired, it finds a clump of bamboo, a hollow tree or an overhanging rock to provide shelter, and lies down to rest. If it has not wandered far, it may use the same **den** two or more nights in a row. Pandas probably have regular dens that they come back to now and then. Pandas sleep for about ten hours in every 24, and even when they are not sleeping, they like to rest a lot. They usually move slowly, although they do sometimes roll and tumble down hillsides. Despite their heavy, bulky shape, pandas are also very good at climbing trees, using their sharp claws and the extra 'thumb' on their front paws to help them grip the branches. They may climb a tree to escape if they feel unsafe, or to take a look at the landscape around them.

Unlike some other types of bears, pandas do not sleep for long periods in the winter, since they can eat bamboo all year round. However, they do move higher up the mountains in summer, when it is too warm for them lower down, and back down in winter when the colder weather comes.

# Reproduction

Giant pandas take six years – longer than most other animals – to grow into mature adults that can **reproduce**. A female usually raises one cub at a time, and looks after it for up to two years before she is ready to **mate** again. This means that pandas reproduce very slowly, and a panda with a young cub is quite a rare sight.

Even when she has reached adulthood, there are only a few weeks every spring when a female panda can become **pregnant**. During this **breeding season**, females give off a special scent and make loud bleating calls to let males know they are ready to mate. Sometimes several different males come to find one female. While she waits up a tree, they may growl at each other, or even fight, until one has managed to chase the others away. Then the male and female play together, rolling around and biting each other gently before mating.

As soon as they have mated, the female runs away, or growls at the male to chase him off her **territory**. The female gives birth and raises her young by herself.

A mother panda hugs and feeds her cub as they sit in the snow.

### Panda family names

As with other animals, there are specific names for male, female and young pandas. Adult male pandas are called boars and females are known as sows, just like male and female pigs. Young pandas are called cubs.

*This tiny panda cub is just one day old. It is very small and has not yet grown its familiar black-and-white fur.*

## Giving birth

A female panda is pregnant for around three to five months. When the mother's cubs are ready to be born, she finds a safe **den**, such as a cave or a hollow tree, and lines it with bits of bark and bamboo. There she gives birth to one or two tiny, pink cubs. (Sometimes there are three cubs, but this is very rare.) As soon as a panda cub is born, it starts squeaking and crying. The mother picks it up carefully using her special extra thumb, and feeds it on milk from her body.

## Only room for one

If there is more than one cub, the mother still only feeds and cares for one of them, usually the bigger one. The smaller cub starves and dies. Scientists think this may happen because it makes more sense for the mother to concentrate all her efforts on caring for one cub, feeding it and keeping it safe, especially if there might be a shortage of food.

Mothers have sometimes been spotted in the wild looking after two cubs instead of one. This could be because they have adopted the cub of another panda that has died, or maybe because they do sometimes decide to raise both cubs.

### Tiny cubs

A newborn panda cub is very, very small compared to its parents. At birth, it is just 15 centimetres long and weighs around 120 grams – a thousandth of the weight of an adult panda. Newborn cubs have only a fine coating of white hair and no black markings, and their bodies and tails are long and thin. Like puppies and kittens, baby pandas are born with their eyes closed. They do not open them until they are around six weeks old.

Like a human baby, a panda cub is helpless at first. Its mother cradles it constantly, licking and nuzzling it, and feeding it up to sixteen times a day. When the cub is hungry or wants something, it cries and squeals just as a human baby does.

A week after it is born, the cub starts to develop dark patches around its eyes. By the age of three weeks it has thick fur with the same black-and-white markings as an adult. After its eyes have opened, at around six weeks old, it starts to crawl, and by three months it can walk easily.

*Four-month-old panda twins rolling and playfighting together.*

## Stepping out

At first the mother stays in the **den** with her cub, but when it is about four weeks old she starts to take it out with her when she goes looking for food. She carries the cub in one paw and seems to walk on the knuckles of that paw. She can also hold the cub in her mouth, as most bears do. Cubs start eating bamboo when they are about one year of age. As the cub grows bigger and stronger, it starts to walk on its own and learns to follow its mother. Older panda cubs love to play. They roll around, slide and tumble down steep slopes and climb on their mother's back.

However, the mother still has to keep a close eye on her cub. Although few animals will attack an adult panda, **predators** such as snow leopards and wild dogs sometimes hunt and eat young pandas.

## Leaving home

By the time it is between eighteen months and two years old, a panda cub is nearly the size of an adult, and is ready to leave home. Although it will not be old enough to reproduce until it is about six, it can now survive on its own, leaving its mother to raise new cubs.

Pandas are usually born in late summer or autumn, so a cub reaches the age of eighteen months in early spring. It then moves away from its mother to find its own **territory**. At this age, the young panda may come across other young pandas who are also looking for territories, and spend some time playing with them. Only when they are older will they become completely **solitary** and live by themselves.

## panda lifespans

Females can keep giving birth until they are between twelve and fourteen years old, so a female could have as many as five cubs in her lifetime. However pandas can live much longer – up to 25 years in the wild. In **captivity**, some pandas have lived to be over 30 years old.

These young pandas are one year old, and are big and strong enough to play and chase each other up trees.

In 1984, the giant panda was added to the official list of endangered **species**, under the USA's Endangered Species Act. In 1994, it was classified as endangered on the international list of endangered and threatened species run by the IUCN, the World Conservation Union. Since the 1960s, it had only been listed as 'rare'.

American tourists visiting China watch a mother and baby panda playing together at Beijing Zoo.

To become officially endangered, a species has to be in danger of **extinction** in all or a main part of its natural **range**. Once a species is officially endangered or threatened, it is protected by international laws, such as those against trading in endangered animals' body parts.

## A critical time

Being endangered is not just about the population of a species falling and falling until there are none left. Instead, the number of individual animals of any species needs to stay above a certain number in order for the species to survive. This minimum level of animals is called a 'critical mass'. For most species, the critical mass is at least several hundred animals. Some wildlife experts think that no population of wild animals is safe unless it contains around 500 individuals.

Although there are around a thousand giant pandas left, most live in tiny groups, numbering no more than around 150 animals in each **isolated** area. Panda experts think this is one reason why it is so hard for pandas to increase their numbers. Each population is so small, it is very hard for a panda to find a **mate** from a different family. In fact, even with their current numbers, giant pandas are right on the brink of extinction.

## People and pandas

Today, people around the world regard the panda as a lovable creature. People are also aware that pandas are endangered. In zoos, pandas are among the most popular animals and draw the biggest crowds, especially when they have cubs. For all these reasons, an image of a panda was chosen as the logo, or symbol, of the **WWF** when it was founded in 1961. However people are still the main reason why panda numbers are falling.

## Falling too far

Endangered species can become destined for extinction, even while there are still quite a few of them left alive. Many species in the world today, such as the baiji, or Chinese river dolphin, are now below their critical mass and will probably die out in the wild. Then their only hope is to be **bred** in **captivity** and released back into the wild at a future date.

The baiji, or Chinese river dolphin, is another endangered species of the region. Unfortunately the baiji is already doomed to extinction in the wild.

There are two main ways in which people cause problems for giant pandas. The first is **habitat loss**. This happens when people destroy the panda's natural **habitat** – mountain bamboo forests – to make space for their farms, towns and roads. When they do not have enough space or a proper supply of their natural food, it is hard for pandas to survive.

Many animals need a large amount of space to live in. They have to be able to move around to find food, meet a **mate** and escape from danger. In the past, large wild animals such as tigers, leopards and giant pandas were spread out over huge areas, and each individual had plenty of space.

## A population explosion

However, in the last few hundred years, the human population has exploded, and people have now taken over vast areas of land that used to be **wilderness**. China has the biggest population of any country in the world – 1.3 billion – and it increased fastest in the second half of the 20th century. All these extra people needed land to live on and grow food on, so they moved into areas that had previously been uninhabited.

*This Chinese mountain village is on the edge of the panda's bamboo forest habitat. You can see how the villagers' farmland has taken over some of the hillside.*

*Workers preparing bamboo to be pulped in a paper factory.*

When people first started to clear mountain forests, they did not always realize how dangerous this would be for pandas and other wild animals. It has only been in the last few decades that we have started to understand how habitat loss affects wild animal **species**.

## A useful plant

Besides being the panda's favourite food, bamboo is used in China to make buildings, furniture, paper and many other things.

## Gone forever

Unfortunately, large areas of mountain forest have now been lost, and it is very difficult to replace them. On hillsides, trees and plants such as bamboo hold soil in place. Once they are cut down, the rain washes some of the soil away, making it hard for those plant species to grow there again. Recreating wild forest areas can also mean moving local people out of the homes and farms they now depend on.

## Disappearing bamboo

In China, bamboo forests have been disappearing for centuries, and in the last few decades they have been cut down faster than ever. As well as being removed to make space for human farms and settlements, the forests where pandas live are sometimes chopped down for the **conifer** wood and bamboo. All this has meant that, since the early 1970s, the area of wild, natural panda habitat has shrunk by more than 50 per cent.

# Saving giant panda habitats

Over the past few decades, scientists, governments and wildlife charities have learned how **habitat loss** affects giant pandas. Now they are working together to try to stop any more panda **habitat** from disappearing. Where possible, they are also trying to reverse habitat loss, by taking over developed areas and turning them back into forests. This is one of the most important things we can do to save the giant panda.

The best way to save an area of natural panda habitat is to make it into a **reserve** – a special area where wildlife is protected by law. In a reserve, it is illegal to chop down trees or other plants, build houses or farms, or disturb wild animals. China now has more than 30 reserves specially designed to give giant pandas a safe place to live. In fact, almost all the pandas that still live in the wild are found in these reserves.

## The Wolong Reserve

The biggest and most famous panda reserve is the Wolong (which means 'sleepy dragon') Reserve, in northwestern **Sichuan**. It was set up in the 1970s and covers an area of just over 2000 square kilometres. As well as being home to around a hundred wild pandas, it has a research and **breeding** station where scientists can study pandas and breed them in **captivity**.

*This photo of part of the Wolong Reserve shows the kind of habitat that suits pandas best: steep, mountainous terrain, with thick forests and plenty of water.*

# Alternatives to logging

In 1998 the Chinese government banned commercial **logging** in natural forests in the southwest of the country. Since logging was made illegal, many former logging companies have begun working with **WWF** to learn how to use forest resources without harming the environment. The companies have received money from the Chinese government to protect and maintain forests like the ones that they used to cut down.

Some of the old logging companies are now hoping to set up new kinds of businesses that will not harm pandas and their environment. Encouraging tourism can be dangerous, as large numbers of people visiting an area can destroy it, when companies start building enormous hotels and restaurants, roads and airports. A more sympathetic approach is to encourage **ecotourism**, and this is what local companies have decided to do. They hope that ecotourism will help **conserve** the forests and help local people find work.

A young panda relaxes on a bench at the Wolong Reserve, surrounded by visiting tourists.

In northern Sichuan, the Wanglang Nature Reserve is a protected area that is the home of many rare endangered **species**, including over 30 giant pandas. Tourist numbers are increasing rapidly from a total of 1000 tourists in 1997 to 20,000 tourists in 2002. The challenge is to make sure that so many tourists do not harm the environment and the animals they have come to visit. WWF is now helping to train tour guides to understand how to promote tourism responsibly.

## Bamboo corridors

A big problem for pandas is **habitat fragmentation** – being divided up into small, **isolated** populations. So there are now plans to join some panda groups together by planting long 'corridors' of bamboo to connect different panda areas. The pandas should be able to move easily to and fro, finding food as they go.

# Giant panda poaching

The second main way people harm giant pandas is by hunting them. Human beings have always regarded pandas as special and even magical. In ancient China, they were highly valued for their fur, because it is very warm and waterproof. It was also used to make bedding and cloaks. Wealthy emperors would present their favourite courtiers or their grandest guests with panda skins as gifts.

## Panda 'magic'

One reason people want to buy panda skins is because of a traditional belief that they have magical powers. According to old Chinese folklore, if you sleep on the skin of a giant panda, you will be protected from ghosts and you will have magical dreams that will predict your future. Old beliefs like this can be very powerful. Many other animals, such as sea turtles, tigers and rhinoceroses, have become endangered because people believe their body parts have special properties or magical powers, and so will pay a lot of money for them.

*This is part of a giant panda's pelt, or skin. It was found when police arrested a group of smugglers in China in 2001.*

▶

*A market booth in Myanmar full of animal parts for sale, many from endangered species.*

More recently, pandas were killed as trophies. Hunters wanted to take home a panda skin, or have a stuffed panda in their house. In the late 19th and early 20th centuries, many pandas were also killed by scientists, so that they could take panda body parts home to study them, or display them in museums.

People have continued to hunt and kill pandas for their skins and as a sport. In the early 20th century, this seriously reduced panda numbers. When there were plenty of pandas, panda numbers could recover more easily. But now, there are so few pandas that killing just one of them makes it more likely that the **species** will die out altogether.

## Killing for money

It is now illegal to kill a panda, but panda skins can still fetch high prices on the **black market**, so **poaching** continues today. Despite laws against poaching, there are still a few people in the world who will pay a lot of money for giant panda skins. One skin can fetch several thousand pounds – more money than most Chinese farmers can earn in their whole lives. So it is not surprising that some poor farmers in China still think it is worth the risk to set snares and traps for pandas, in the hope of gaining instant wealth.

As well as being targeted by poachers, pandas also risk being caught in traps set for other wild animals, such as other types of bears and musk deer.

How can people be stopped from killing giant pandas? Of course, the first step is to make panda **poaching** illegal and to impose severe punishments on those who break the law. Panda hunting has been illegal in China since the 1960s. Even so, poaching continued out of control. Then in 1987 the Chinese government made the penalties much stricter. Killing a panda, or smuggling a panda skin, became punishable by a minimum prison sentence of 20 years, or the death sentence. Although judges do not usually impose the death penalty, people can still be sent to jail for life for killing pandas. There are also international laws against trading in the skins or other body parts of endangered **species**. So even outside China, being caught with a panda pelt is a serious crime.

It is hard to get the balance right, however, between strict laws and unreasonable punishments. Many people feel that a death sentence for poaching pandas actually makes it harder to protect them. People will be less likely to turn someone in who might be put to death.

*A guard at Wanglang Nature Reserve in Sichuan Province. A panda reserve guard is always on the look-out for pandas, as well as poachers and illegal **loggers**.*

## Panda visits

Since people have started to take over more areas that used to be occupied by pandas, they have ended up living in closer contact with pandas than before. There have even been several reports of pandas wandering into villages, farms and other human settlements. According to one of these tales, in 1983 a giant panda walked into a farmer's home, where it ate a bowl of rice and had a rest on the bed before leaving.

# Panda police

The problem with laws like this is that they have to be enforced. Although panda **reserves** have rangers and wardens who watch out for poachers, it is very difficult to keep watch over wild pandas, or to catch people who might be trying to poach them, because their mountain forest **habitat** is so dense, remote and hard to travel in. It is also hard to track down panda skins once they have left China. They are not sold in normal shops, but on the **black market**, usually in secret locations.

The first step for panda reserves is to hire more rangers. Rangers also need to be trained. Presently, many rangers are low-paid, and lack equipment and even uniforms that would help them tackle poachers with confidence. Charities like the Panda Trust have helped rangers at Wolong, China's biggest giant panda reserve, by providing equipment such as uniforms, rucksacks, video cameras and radio telephones. The charity has also funded training courses for rangers.

At the BaiShuiHe Nature Reserve in **Sichuan**, managers plan to build five ranger stations. While the Chinese government is providing funds to build the ranger stations in the reserve, funds are still needed to pay for the rangers.

Poaching has not been stamped out, but it is becoming rarer, and is not as much of a problem as it was in the 1980s and 1990s. But making this happen requires constant effort and funds. Strict laws, education programmes and reward schemes have to stay in place to keep pandas as safe as possible.

*The background in this picture of a panda gives you an idea of how hard it is to track poachers in such steep and wild terrain.*

# Helping local people help pandas

Changing the attitudes of local people and businesses is essential if the giant panda is to be saved. As well as making laws, the Chinese government is now working to educate its people about the plight of giant pandas. When they learn that the panda is endangered, and that there is a huge international struggle to save it, local people are less likely to want to kill one.

Besides setting up **reserves**, the Chinese government is trying to encourage local people to help pandas when they can. It sends teachers to explain to people that pandas are rare and should be protected. Farmers are encouraged to feed hungry pandas who wander on to their land. They are also taught how to grow crops such as mushrooms, which can grow among the bamboo and forest trees. When farmers grow other crops they normally have to cut down the forest first to make space for them.

*Schoolchildren in China learning about the environment and the importance of saving endangered **species**.*

*A farmer crossing his bamboo fields near the Wolong Panda Research Centre. Conservation has to be sensitive to the needs of local people.*

## Rewarding people

The Chinese government also pays local people to help pandas. The government rewards people, for example, for feeding a panda that is starving, or for protecting a panda that wanders into a village or on to farmland. Although not as high as the price of a dead panda, these cash payments are still high compared to a farmer's normal income. So people have started to regard living pandas as valuable, and are keen to help them when they can.

## New approaches

The government is also helping local people in other ways. It has extended electricity cables to some mountain villages so that villagers can use electric heating instead of chopping down trees for firewood. There are even rescue teams that look for pandas that have run out of bamboo, catch them and transport them to other areas where there is still plenty of bamboo to eat.

To try to give the pandas back some of their old **habitat**, people from some farms and towns have even been moved away from the mountain forests, and some fields are being replanted with bamboo. Two different types of bamboo are planted in each area, so that if one type flowers and dies back, the other should remain to provide food for pandas. Meanwhile, scientists are developing new fertilizers and plant food that can make bamboo grow faster, in order to recreate panda habitat as quickly as possible.

Thanks to awareness schemes and international **conservation** efforts, most Chinese people now see the giant panda as a national treasure and a symbol of China.

It is not just human activity that threatens giant pandas. They are also at risk because they are so **specialized** – **adapted** to a very particular **habitat** and lifestyle, and a very specific diet of bamboo. These special needs mean that changes in **climate** or plant life can cause huge problems for pandas.

## Bamboo die-offs

One problem with relying on bamboo for a food supply is that, every few years, large areas of bamboo flowers die back and disappear for a while before starting to grow again. When this happens, pandas have to find a new supply of bamboo. In the past, this was not such a big problem as it is today, because when one area of bamboo died, the pandas could simply move to another area and feed on a different bamboo **species**. Because groups of pandas now live in small, **isolated** areas, cut off from each other by farmland and towns, a bamboo flowering can spell panda starvation.

## Panda predators

Apart from people, there are not really any **predators** that hunt and kill adult pandas. However, panda cubs are at risk from hunting animals such as snow leopards and wolves. Again, when pandas weren't so rare, this wasn't such a big problem. Some cubs did get eaten, but there were enough wild pandas to make up the numbers. Today each panda community really needs every cub to survive in order to keep its population steady.

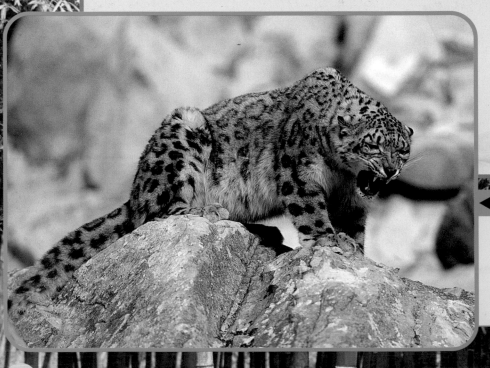

*A snow leopard revealing its sharp meat-eater's teeth. Snow leopards are now more likely than ever to kill and eat panda cubs.*

Unfortunately, natural predators are more of a risk than ever. One reason is that the predators themselves are in trouble. The snow leopard, for example, is seriously endangered. Like the panda, it suffers from **habitat loss**, and its favourite prey animals, such as wild goats and sheep, are disappearing as farms take over their habitats and food sources. This makes it even more likely that a snow leopard, hungry and searching for any food it can find, will be forced to snatch a baby panda.

## Climate change

While disasters caused by bad weather, such as floods, have killed pandas in the past, future climate change could be even deadlier for pandas. Global warming could also have an impact. If world temperatures continue to rise because of air pollution, animals that are only comfortable in cold climates will be at risk. Higher temperatures could be harmful to pandas as they run out of suitable high-altitude forest that remains cool enough for them to live in.

*Villagers construct a dyke to protect the giant panda **reserve** in the Qin Ling mountains of China's Shaanxi province from floods.*

## The 1970s bamboo famine

One of the biggest bamboo flowerings in recent times happened in the late 1970s, in the northern part of China's **Sichuan** province. Sichuan makes up an important part of the giant panda's **range**, and when the bamboo died off, hundreds of pandas were left to starve. This disaster killed many pandas and seriously damaged the panda population. However, it also helped to wake people up to the plight of the panda, and kick-started panda **conservation** efforts around the world. From the early 1980s onwards, the Chinese government increased its efforts to help pandas, and teamed up with international conservation groups to study, monitor and **breed** pandas.

# Giant panda campaigns

People have been aware of the giant panda's problems for about 50 years, since the Chinese government began to monitor panda populations in the 1950s. However, **conservation** efforts really took off in the 1970s, when the Chinese started to build panda research stations and set aside large amounts of land for panda **reserves**.

As the panda's problems became more widely known around the world, conservation organizations from other countries began to work with the Chinese on panda-saving campaigns. The biggest of these was **WWF**. This organization, started in 1961, was originally called the World Wildlife Fund. It later changed its name to the Worldwide Fund for Nature, and today it is known simply as WWF. It works to protect endangered wildlife **species** and their **habitats**, through schemes such as sending scientists to study endangered animals, raising awareness about endangered species, and running adopt-an-animal programmes.

This is the modern version of the famous WWF panda logo.

## The panda logo

The panda has been the logo of the WWF for over 40 years. It was originally based on sketches of Chi Chi, a panda who lived at London Zoo in the 1960s, drawn by the British naturalist Gerald Watterson. The famous British naturalist Sir Peter Scott, one of the founders of the WWF, studied the drawings and designed the famous logo. It has been changed several times to keep it looking modern. Over the years, the logo has helped to make the panda one of the world's most easily recognized animals.

## Panda plan

In 1980, WWF started to work closely with the Chinese government to develop a panda protection plan. Together they have arranged many panda-studying trips so that Chinese and foreign scientists can work together to count pandas and learn more about what they need to survive. WWF also helped to build the world's biggest panda research station and **captive breeding** centre at the Wolong Reserve in **Sichuan**. Today, it continues to campaign for pandas, paying for training for reserve wardens and guards, and proposing new ideas such as the bamboo corridor scheme. WWF also helps train local businesses to find ways for local people to make money without damaging pandas and their habitat.

## Famous pandas

Now and then pandas have made headline news. Every time this happens it helps remind people about pandas and their plight. Su Lin was the first panda to be exported alive from China. He was taken to live in a zoo in Chicago, USA, in 1936. In 1963 Li-Li became the first panda to give birth in **captivity**, to Ming-Ming, at Beijing Zoo in China. In the 1960s London Zoo's Chi Chi made headline news when she was 'engaged' to An An, from Moscow Zoo. Chang Chang, the world's oldest panda, died in 2002 at Jinan Zoo in China, at around 35 years of age.

A young WWF volunteer. Her job is to take visitors on the trail of giant pandas in the Qin Ling mountains of Shaanxi Province, China.

# Giant panda research

Research means studying something and trying to find out more about it. Several different types of scientists carry out research into giant pandas and their lifestyle, **habitat**, behaviour and animal relatives. They include zoologists, who study animals; ecologists, who study habitats and the wildlife that lives in them; and geneticists, who study the **genes** and **DNA** of living things. Genes are the microscopic 'building blocks' of life that make each individual different from the next.

When animals are endangered, studying them closely is very important. It helps us to understand what surroundings they need, how they **reproduce** and what kinds of food they can survive on. Panda scientists also do research to find out how many pandas there are and how seriously they are endangered.

Researching pandas, especially in the wild, is hard work. Scientists have to go on long **field trips**, trekking and camping in the forest for several weeks, to follow pandas and find out information about them. China also has special panda research stations where scientists can keep pandas **captive** while they study them.

A scientist uses a microscope to study **cells** from a giant panda's body. You can see them on the screen on the right.

## Panda clues

A lot of panda research is done without even seeing a panda. Instead, scientists look for tracks and signs that reveal where pandas have been and what they have been doing. They include panda footprints, chewed bamboo plants, scratch marks on trees, and panda droppings. These are long and pointed, and the pointed end shows the direction in which the panda has headed. Using signs like these, experts can follow a panda's movements and activities. They can also use them to track down and catch a panda for further research.

*These scientists are radio-tracking a panda. They are holding up antennae to collect radio signals from a radio collar fitted to a giant panda somewhere in the area.*

## Radio-tracking

To keep tabs on exactly where a panda is, scientists use radio-tracking. They catch a panda, using a dart to inject it with a drug that makes it go to sleep for a short time. Then they fit it with a special collar that gives off radio signals. When the panda is set free, a receiver picks up the signals and shows where the panda is. Scientists can use this information to find the panda again quickly, or to map the way it moves around its **territory** and habitat.

### The Wolong Research Station

China's biggest panda **reserve**, Wolong, also has a scientific research station. There, scientists can keep the pandas they are studying in a safe enclosure. They also run a **captive breeding** programme. Parts of the station are open to the public, who come to watch the pandas being fed and to see mother pandas with their newborn cubs. The station also has science laboratories and living quarters for visiting scientists.

Around 140 giant pandas live in zoos and research stations around the world. Most of them are in China, but there are also pandas in Japan, Mexico, Germany, the UK, and in San Diego, Atlanta and Washington DC in the USA. In the past, China often 'rented' pandas out to foreign zoos, and used the money to pay for wild panda protection schemes. This may be revived as a way to help pay for panda **conservation** in the future.

Through the 1970s and 1980s, pandas became more and more popular with the public. **Captive breeding** programmes took off, and whenever a captive panda gave birth it became headline news. People flocked to zoos to see the giant pandas and their cubs. In 1987, when San Diego Zoo borrowed two pandas for a six-month stay, attendance at the zoo increased by a third.

*Schoolchildren crowd around the enclosure of Shuan Shuan, a 16-year-old female panda at Tokyo Zoo in Japan.*

## Captive breeding

Captive breeding – breeding animals in zoos or breeding stations – is often used to try to increase the numbers of an endangered **species** and help it to survive. Unfortunately for pandas, they don't breed very well in captivity. It is hard to persuade captive pandas to **mate** at all, and even if a female does manage to give birth, the cubs often die when they are very young. Experts think this may be because giant pandas, especially males, suffer a lot of stress when they are kept in captivity, as they naturally prefer to live alone and far away from people. Since panda captive breeding programmes began, several hundred pandas have been born in captivity, but less than a quarter of them have survived to adulthood.

These eight panda cubs, four sets of twins, were all born at the Wolong **Reserve** as a result of artificial insemination.

## Getting it right

Over the years, however, zookeepers and panda experts have developed ways to help pandas **reproduce** in captivity, and to help the cubs survive. One way is to use artificial insemination. This is when **cells** are taken from the male's body and injected into the female's body, so that the pandas don't have to mate. Then, when the female gives birth to her two cubs, zookeepers take away the smaller cub, which would normally be left to die, and raise it themselves. This means that both cubs have a chance of surviving. With methods like these, breeders have become much more successful in recent years. Cubs born in the captive breeding programme at Wolong, for example, now have almost a 100 per cent chance of survival.

### A taste for metal

The ancient Chinese studied pandas and their behaviour. For example, a geography text from around 500 BC described them as animals that like to eat metal. Pandas don't really eat metal, but they do like the taste of it. Panda scientists and zookeepers have noticed that after eating their food from metal bowls, pandas often lick and taste the bowls long after the food is all gone. The actual reason for this is not known, although some believe that pandas can taste certain elements in the metal that are **nutritionally** important for them.

Will the giant panda die out? Experts don't all agree. Some say that along with other very endangered **species**, such as the tiger, the panda could be **extinct** within 20 years. Others think that the panda will probably survive at least throughout the 21st century, and maybe longer.

Although the panda population is small, it has now been stable for around 20 years, and doesn't seem to be shrinking. Workers at some panda **reserves** in China have reported that they are now seeing more wild pandas than they used to, suggesting that in some areas, pandas might be starting to increase their numbers at last.

*A worker at the Wolong Centre feeds twin panda cubs on specially prepared milk.*

## Luckier than some

Pandas are still threatened by **habitat loss** and **poaching**, but they do not suffer from some of the problems that face many other endangered species. For example, they are not usually hunted for their meat, and they are not at risk from the dangerous **viruses** which can harm some other animals. The area where they live is relatively peaceful and not troubled by wars, which cause problems for other endangered species, such as gorillas in Africa. On top of all this, the giant panda is at the centre of one of the biggest, most expensive and most famous **conservation** campaigns the world has ever seen. It enjoys massive popularity worldwide, and millions of people around the world support efforts to save it. As long as those efforts continue, the giant panda does have a chance of escaping extinction.

## Scientific solutions

Besides protecting wild pandas and running **captive breeding** programmes, conservationists and scientists are working on new methods and inventions to help pandas in the future. Some scientists are working with bamboo to see if they can develop new faster-growing types. **Satellite** technology is also being developed to track pandas in their natural habitat, and to observe areas of wild bamboo to record when they flower and die. In zoos, scientists and zookeepers are working on panda **nutrition** to find out what kind of diet gives cubs the best chance of surviving. Before long, scientists may even be able to **clone** pandas.

*Dolly the sheep, the first **mammal** to be successfully cloned, shown here with her own lamb, Bonnie.*

## Panda cloning

Cloning means making an animal that is an exact copy of another animal. A cloned animal is made by taking an animal **cell**, and inserting its **DNA** into an egg cell from a female. In 1996, scientists in Scotland successfully created a cloned sheep, named Dolly, and since then several other types of **mammals** have been cloned. Conservationists soon realized they might be able to use cloning to increase the numbers of endangered species, and now scientists at the Chinese Academy of Sciences in Beijing have started work on a panda cloning programme. They plan to implant the cloned panda cell in the womb of another animal, such as a bear. However there are still problems with cloning. Cloned animals often die soon after birth or suffer from diseases in later life. Cloning might one day be able to help the giant panda, but only if these problems are solved.

# How can you help?

If you want to join in the international effort to save the giant panda, there are lots of things you can do. It's easy to become a member of a **conservation** group or charity, such as **WWF** or the Panda Trust. By paying a subscription fee, members of the charity can help to fund its conservation campaigns and help to pay its scientists. You might also receive a magazine, a badge and stickers or fact sheets when you join.

If the subscription fee is too expensive for you on your own, why not ask if your family or your class at school can join instead? Or you could organize something like a sponsored walk or charity concert to raise money to send to a conservation campaign.

You can also support charities like WWF by buying Christmas cards, T-shirts and other goods from them. WWF, for example, has a catalogue full of wildlife T-shirts and other goods, many of them featuring pandas.

*Buying WWF panda merchandise, like this cuddly toy, helps WWF fund its panda projects in China.*

## Could you be a panda expert?

Giant pandas are so rare and well-protected, it is very hard for a normal member of the public to see them in the wild. But if you are really interested in pandas, you could become a scientist, a zookeeper or a conservationist, and then you might end up working with pandas yourself. If you think you might want to do this, it will help if you pick subjects like biology, chemistry or general science at school, and consider studying biology or zoology at university.

An 'adopt a panda' box from WWF. On the front of the box is the name of the particular panda that you have adopted.

## Adopt a panda

When you adopt a panda, it doesn't come to live with you! Instead you send some money to help look after a panda in a zoo, **reserve** or **breeding** station. In return, you get a photo of your panda and letters about how he or she is doing. Adopting an endangered animal such as a panda is a great way to help wildlife and find out more about animals and conservation at the same time.

## Where's your nearest panda?

Visting **captive** pandas is another way to help zoos care for them. You can use the internet to find out the locations of zoos that have pandas – there might even be a panda in your nearest city. If not, you could look out for zoos when you are on holiday.

With a little luck and a lot of money, scientific knowledge and hard work, we could help the beautiful giant panda to recover its numbers, and live in safety and **solitude** in its natural mountain home.

# Glossary

**adapted**  suited to a particular habitat or type of food

**black market**  illegal trade that is kept secret from governments and the police

**breed**  mate and reproduce

**breeding season**  time of year when an animal species is ready to reproduce

**camouflage**  markings and patterns that help an animal blend in with its surroundings

**captive breeding**  helping animals that are kept in zoos or reserves to breed

**captivity**  living in a zoo, cage or other enclosed space

**cell**  tiny unit of living matter. Different cells help animals and plants to complete different tasks, such as breathing, growth, digestion and movement.

**census**  population count

**climate**  weather conditions and temperature range of a particular part of the world

**clone**  animal created by copying another animal's DNA

**conifer**  tree that produces seeds in cones

**conservation**  trying to protect nature and wildlife from being destroyed

**den**  place where an animal makes a home or shelter, such as a cave or hollow tree

**digest**  break down food into useful chemicals that the body can use for growth and energy

**digit**  finger, thumb or toe

**DNA**  (deoxyribonucleic acid) a chemical inside a cell that forms instructions called genes, telling the cell how to work and grow

**ecotourism**  type of tourism that involves visiting a place especially to see the plants and animals that live there

**extinction**  when a species dies out and stops existing forever

**fibre**  tough, hard-to-digest substance found in plants

**field trip**  trip scientists or students go on to study things in the real world, instead of in a laboratory

**genes**  instructions inside the cells of living things that tell them how to work

**gland**  organ that releases a particular substance that helps the body work

**habitat**   surroundings where a particular species lives, such as a forest

**habitat fragmentation**   division of a habitat into small, isolated areas

**habitat loss**   disappearance of areas of a natural habitat

**isolate**   cut off from others

**logging**   industry that cuts down trees on a large scale for money

**mammal**   any warm-blooded animal that feeds its young on milk from its body

**mate**   when a male and female animal get together to produce young; a partner of the opposite sex

**missionary**   someone who travels abroad to spread a religious message in the hope of converting people to that religion

**nutrition**   food that contains chemicals useful for living and growing

**poaching**   illegal hunting of wild animals

**predator**   animal that hunts and eats other animals

**pregnant**   when a female has babies or eggs growing inside her

**pupils**   dark holes in the middle of the eyes that let light in

**range**   overall area where a wildlife species is found

**reproduction**   scientific name for mating and breeding

**reserve**   area of land set aside for wildlife to live in safety

**satellite**   spacecraft that orbits, or travels around, the Earth. Some satellites can collect data about the Earth and beam it to computers on the ground.

**Sichuan**   region in central southern China

**solitary**   alone

**specialized**   specially designed to cope with an unusual habitat or lifestyle

**species**   scientific name for a particular kind of plant, animal or other living thing

**territory**   area of land that an animal lives in and guards for itself

**virus**   tiny germ. Some types of viruses cause serious diseases.

**vitamin**   substance present in food which is important for normal growth and nutrition

**wilderness**   wild, natural areas of land that have not been taken over by humans

**WWF**   Worldwide Fund for Nature, a wildlife charity that was founded in London in 1961

## Conservation groups and websites

### Worldwide Fund for Nature, or WWF
*www.panda.org*
International charity that takes action to conserve threatened species, tackle global threats to the environment and seek sustaintable solutions for the benefit of people and nature.

### The Panda Trust
*www.panda-trust.org.uk*
Organization devoted to pandas that funds equipment for rangers at Wolong Reserve, as well as other projects.

### Pandas International
*www.pandasinternational.org*
Find out how to adopt a giant panda at the Pandas International website.

### Enchanted Learning: All About Pandas
*www.enchantedlearning.com/subjects/mammals/panda/*
A fun site with lots of useful information and panda pictures.

### Junglewalk.com
*www.junglewalk.com/frames.asp* and click on 'Pandas'
At this site you can see panda videos and listen to panda sounds.

### University of Michigan Museum of Zoology
*http://animaldiversity.ummz.umich.edu/site/accounts/information/Ailuropoda_melanoleuca.html*
Detailed scientific facts about the giant panda.

# Books

*Bears and Pandas (Nature Watch),* Michael Bright
(Lorenz Books, 2000)

*Giant Panda (Natural World),* Malcolm Penny
(Hodder Children's Books, 2000)

*The Giant Panda,* David Taylor
(Boxtree, 1990)

*Green Alert: Vanishing Forests,* Lim Cheng Puay
(Raintree, 2004)

*The Last Panda,* George Schaller
(University of Chicago Press, 1994)

*The Secret World of Pandas,* eds Byron Preiss and Gao Xueyu
(Harry N. Abrams Inc., 1990)

# Index